Matthew

**This Isn't the Apocalypse
We Hoped For**

So great to meet you
"not-across-the-coffee-bar"!
Enjoy!

THIS ISN'T THE APOCALYPSE WE HOPED FOR

Al Rempel

CAITLIN PRESS

01 02 03 04 05 06 18 17 16 15 14 13

Caitlin Press Inc.
8100 Alderwood Road,
Halfmoon Bay, BC V0N 1Y1
www.caitlin-press.com

Text design by Kathleen Fraser.
Cover design by Vici Johnstone.
Cover photo by John Lund, Getty Images #102680111.
Author photo by Jayson Hencheroff, Focal Point Studios.
Edited by Elizabeth Bachinsky.
Printed in Canada

Caitlin Press Inc. acknowledges financial support from
the Government of Canada through the Canada Book
Fund and the Canada Council for the Arts, and from the
Province of British Columbia through the British Columbia
Arts Council and the Book Publisher's Tax Credit.

Canada Council Conseil des Arts
for the Arts   du Canada

BRITISH COLUMBIA
ARTS COUNCIL
An agency of the Province of British Columbia

Library and Archives Canada Cataloguing in Publication

Rempel, Al, 1969–
   This isn't the apocalypse we hoped for / Al Rempel.

Poems.
ISBN 978-1-927575-08-6

   I. Title.

PS8635.E497T45 2013   C811'.6   C2013-900321-5

for Eloise

who will inherit this earth

"If it walks like apocalypse. If it squawks like armageddon."

— *Dennis Lee,* Testament

CONTENTS

Lunch at Eleven-O-One   11
We Love Bananas   12
Butter   13
Table Setting for Six   14
Leaving the Terminal   15
On the Way to the Dump   16
Silver & Blue   17
Kiss Her   18
Right through the Earth   19
Huntingdon Man   20
In Rain, In Love   21
Survival Kit   22
Within the Hour   24
Bring Me My Sky Canoe   25
Shamrock Road, Prince George, BC   26
Salmon Forest   27
The Song in her Head   28
Hymn for the Dandelions   29
At the Dock, Briefly   30
Turning the Corner   31
Out of the Dust   32
Chock-a-Block   33
Overlooking Highland Drive   34
Beyond the Ridge   35
On the Hart Highway   36
Streets are not the Map   37
This is It   38
Blind Bird   39
This Isn't the Apocalypse We Hoped For   40
Proximity   41
Deconstructing Esso   42
Urban Dreams   43

The Face of the Deep   44
Xylophobia   45
This Day, All Day, the Trees Are Drapes   46
Grandstanding on the Boulevard   47
Sunday Morning Drive   48
Have a Bath   49
A Novel in Excerpts   50
    Chapter One   50
    Chapter Eleven   51
    Chapter Twelve   52
    Afterword   53
Night Psalm   54
Half-Past Christmas   55
As We Zigzag Through the Schoolyard Gate   56
And on Earth Above   57
Ain't Gonna Be   60
Looking For   61
Blip-Blip   62
Aftershocks   63
On the Porch   64
Acknowledgements   67
Notes   69

LUNCH AT ELEVEN-O-ONE

the sun slides out as if from a bun
with a restaurant-style pickle
a smear of mustard
and just enough yellow to stain

I fumble with the rest
the crevasses in my car, their accretions —
all the basic building blocks
for a fast-food joint

barely in control of the steering wheel
polished with animal grease
I cruise into another crummy day —
belch quietly into the window

WE LOVE BANANAS

we love bananas. we love the way they taste, we love
how they fill our mouths. we love that they're loaded
with potassium. we love their yellowness. we love how
they peel. we love them the way we love Curious George
and the man with the yellow hat. the way
we love slapstick. the way we used to shoot them
as if they were guns. the way they're cocked
under the supermarket lights. oh yes we love bananas.

here's what we do with bananas. we buy them just
when they're turning yellow. we play the Tarzan
theme song in our heads as we carry them to the car.
we place them in a ceramic bowl and leave them
out with the still life. we forget to eat them and they go
soft. we put them on the top shelf in the freezer.
we throw them out when we can't fit
the box of pizza in. we've already bought more.

BUTTER

o she   dipped her finger in the melted butter
of our breakfast toast   yes I   saw her
spread it on her cheek   above her ·   left eye
and on the bridge of her nose   when she
pushed up her glasses   she said   we eat
with more than just our mouths   no we
won't be defined by the limits of our skin   when we
spend the last fifteen minutes in bed   and she
stretches into me   and she   takes me in
and I   no she   and we   o she —
when we woke up   languid and sleep-soaked
no we   didn't think we'd spend it talking about toast

TABLE SETTING FOR SIX

we sit down at the table
casually rearrange the day's events

even the cloth of rain outside
the exact corners of our napkins

set this down: we smile
but can no longer taste the soil

the eyes of the potatoes untouched
grow ugly clawed protrusions

the rain will peter out, the silver
will slip ahead of the shadows

we'll get up from our places unable
to remember why we were here

LEAVING THE TERMINAL

we're on board
and the ocean rises to meet us.
the men at the gates are left standing with their safety vests on,
recede with social conventions and the rebuke of seagulls.
we should talk about the light —
it's gone.

there had been a flash of orange at sunset
that shot up from the horizon,
then a thin strip of ochre,
then rain.

rain is the darkest dark I know

I can feel my jaw tighten again
and I'm not sure how long it's been this way.
if it makes me look serious, or glum, or worried.
I'm happy, you know
at least I think I am

perhaps skin has the same mechanism
as shrink wrap

your hand on my arm draws me back
not to you, but to the beating rain
which runs rivulets down the ferry windows
lit up in the ferry's strange light

what is it? you ask

it's dark.

ON THE WAY TO THE DUMP

                    the fan
is shattered off its base,
the blades without the will
to turn

                    in this long stretch
uphill, the eskers give way to horizon,
western skies, a play of light
tilting off clouds

                    there's always
a truck. the wind we create
pillages empty boxes;
a mattress is doubled over
at the waist

                    ahead —
sudden brake lights and a quick
dodge. for a moment the sun
fills the interior of our car
and then moves on

SILVER & BLUE

blue   within blue   and silver

    silvery leaves   brighter than blades

       and yet her eyes

flirt   dip your hand   make the water

    make a glove   remind her   quicksilver

       skin of fire

at night   the moon parted   blue steel

    parted the lake   and her eyes

       a wide wider than

KISS HER

the sun is climbing the walls
with thrumoxes and pixets
and buzzlings that blunder

some bits of the picture weave
in and out of the raspberry canes —
the picture that is me.
some are stuffed as insulation
between cedar rafters
and the brick chimney

don't light the fire
don't open the damper

I pulled open a drawer —
out fell a scrap of paper
torn where the sun-motes touched...
half was her, and I hunted the house
until I found another
in the springs of the couch

the crick in my neck is a wonder —
work it out while the cat in his dreams
disassembles the veranda.
the click in my knees is a type of weather
brewing under the kitchen table
with stitchings and lightning-feathers

kiss her in the unawares
kiss her for some cover

RIGHT THROUGH THE EARTH

the rocking chair on its side
I want to say
                        breathing heavily
but it's me gasping, as billions of neutrinos
streak through the roof, then every square inch of me
then the floor, then the slab of petrified wood in the crawl space
— souvenir of our final family vacation together
then right through the earth
and out the other side

I want to see again, its arctic-blue eyes:
my husky, circling in the back of the truck

this isn't how I thought it would end —
with this light scattered off the flies buzzing about
the orange bulb overhead, with a pull chain
lengthened by a string

I want, more than anything
to be upright in my chair again —
for an hour
at least

the comfort
of moving
over familiar scritch-marks on the floor

HUNTINGDON MAN

what kind of man emerges
from under blackberries?

does he find in his dreams
remnants of the Telegraph Trail
where he can rip off the copper wire
from the forest floor?

with his green-glass eyes
in early spring
the ice falling dit-dah
dah-dah-dit-dit down
all around from the insulators
nailed to trees

yesterday was Friday —
should be lots of bottles
in the ditch

the first thing he sees
is a seagull in the rain
white with spotted tail feathers
and a mouth that opens salmon-red

IN RAIN, IN LOVE

the rain falls
through the room
to the roots underneath —
makes the house wider from bottom to top

we step through puddles
having dispensed with umbrellas
watch the water rise
wade between kitchen and bedroom —
it's a wonder
nothing's floating about

o we're tethered
tethered and bright!
red balloons and kites
tied to this mooring

the ripples around my knees
send lovely messages to you —
you send back a wave

sweet jungle of a home:
cockatiels and pleasant hippos splash;
we could easily drown
in this afternoon

SURVIVAL KIT

1.

a plastic straw
slides into the kitchen sink drain
ready to jam up
shards of lettuce and plugs
of leftover spaghetti,
and what doesn't all fit
into the back of a car —
handlebars of mountain bikes
recliners on their sides, strips of wooden trim
tapping the road

and there's overstuffed duffle bags
full of hockey equipment
stickhandling people's legs
at the bus depot,
purses spilling out eyeliners,
pocket squares of envelopes
in worn Mackinaw jackets,
drawers that don't open
because of a ruler, or a pair of salad tongs
catching on from below

desktops awash in icons

2.

keep everything, or nearly, because
you never know, dad's basement
was a hodgepodge, an accumulation,
in drawers and stacked along the floor

up in the joists he slipped dowels
and other long-thin-light things —
this is a partial list, you understand

here's something: every poem written
is a list; and then it happens —
something breaks, something needs
building; this, that, and the other
become necessity

WITHIN THE HOUR

on George St. the workers come at night
dismantle the covered walk
            — sounds of chainsaws singing

a curtain of linked rebar   hangs aimlessly
in front of nothing

under a perforated sky
filled with the terror of starlight
            — we are left to wander

wait to see what   replaces what

BRING ME MY SKY CANOE

a small apology of light
between the clouds

then it evaporates — the sun ogles the hills
the bears continue to hide in the shadows
and we keep driving our cars into the harsh glare

which species will see the second coming?

we could travel in sky canoes
if the air wasn't so thin
or if our canoes were built with feathers and breath

the trees below are perfect.

the sun up here has a way of lighting everything slantwise
strong arm of my paddle —
strong arm of my paddle —
strong arm of my paddle —
take me safely along this ancient and fearful river

SHAMROCK ROAD, PRINCE GEORGE, BC

we saw the unfortunate collisions
crushed into bales, shipping out of town
on long flatbeds and we barely winced,

would rather not see homemade crosses
tapped into the fog near retaining walls,
the faded-black skids, the plastic wreaths

hung up on hydro poles, and at dusk,
the personhood of their shadows
stretching across the slick asphalt —

believed we had achieved levitation
floated so mercifully above the streets

SALMON FOREST
For Ken Belford

& there are holes in the forest

moose-sized holes & bear-sized holes &
holes for things with wings
& for things that slither

& of course holes in the trees
(see the grinning ovoids)
to be read at night after the fire
has licked your eyes clean

but the best-sized holes
are no bigger than a salmon

with a flash of silver
you can go in
(spear-eyed) & under & after

the liquid dark
a second forest

breathe starlight & shadow-wings
& the soft press of absence

underfoot & at your sides

THE SONG IN HER HEAD

butterflies hooded her eyes
but I was sure I saw
something shining inside

her fingernails, just out of reach
kept time
on the thick lacquer finish

not to the song in the room
nor to the one in my head

yes I meant to ask her
but was distracted by the flowers
unfolding all along her collarbone

and my feet, unable to move
because of the grass
sprung up under the table

HYMN FOR THE DANDELIONS

crushed saffron in the palm, buttery breath, orange at the wrists

a yellow to make taxicabs jealous

what we felt under thrust-out chins

lemon punch

bed-bright

bikini bottoms and tops stringing on a line

yellow tanager in the bellybutton, frenetic tongues

god-play in the fields

fistfuls for the vase

AT THE DOCK, BRIEFLY

unsettled near the ocean — all that water
the stink of it and the weight pressing
with the return of the tide — finishes him.

he goes down to the dock; a flat shuffle
and deliberately in the middle — his eyes question
the bright sails, the oversexed motors

and land on an island: such brave stone.
the trees reel in the wind, salt-grass
somehow sprouts — seaweed on its knees

this is as far as he gets — drops down
a coin between the cracks, thinks
I can go now into the safety

of this tourist town, booths at the park,
bundles of fresh-picked herbs; he buys
his fish at the IGA, frozen and filleted

TURNING THE CORNER

a kindness, this ballooning sky, this posse of trees
their willingness to enter, this green

and this scent waylaid on branches, mingled
with a wet handed down in droplets

from one needle cluster to the next — I'll take it —
let's remember how many closed doors we open

in a day, how many packets of light and fray
make us squint and shift our eyes, this life

this brief vision, this kindness, a trapdoor

at the bottom of the brain, a sudden weightlessness
a falling into childhood, a moment of recognition

before the machinery of the mind gets busy —
it is, after all, only a particular chemical concoction

you could one day cook up in a lab, yesterday's mix
got you discomfort and distress, today it happens

to be a kindness — take it, press it close

OUT OF THE DUST

sweet rain, whose ancient memory
mixes water and dust so well
and whom shall we thank?

even on concrete and asphalt
the smell drives us
back to happier times

the hills falling away
seem much more vital
in this diffuse light

CHOCK-A-BLOCK

onslaught of bad songs   turn radio off
parking lot   a Brinks truck   the last spot
insert self   hard right   full stop   lock car
giant flower pot   non-native pink blossoms
exhaust resistant   patio furniture about the knees
accent   speak more clearly   coffee   get going
the ambulance pushy through traffic
panic in the back   a man picks his nose
in the Escalade   keep going   a black plastic bag
gently lifts off a pickup bed   two horns honk
look left   the driver doesn't budge   or shift
the lady wearing her legs   poses
another glance on the sidewalk   shift gears
coffee   try the radio again   James Brown
tap along

o bubblegum-pink washer fluid
        let me drive the way they do on TV
                o god of gearboxes, don't fail me now

OVERLOOKING HIGHLAND DRIVE

sit yourself on this earth
or wait for a new one
forever and ever amen

last week I waited
for a moment to happen —
it never did

there is dust on the shelf
and other places
I can't reach

now to the business of living:
take a breath in
and let one breath out

a longing washed over me
as each star
appeared at night

BEYOND THE RIDGE

the open-mouthed coyote. o moon
do not spare the agony of light
and roundness. the endless stands
of articulated trees

and deeper down, the muscled dark
is firmly attached. moon slither.
root mass. a shape that any moss
can take on. back into

a welcome clearing. o grandfather
come close. you say bog but it smells
of lake. grins with incisive crescents.
with muck on his fur

ON THE HART HIGHWAY

willows still green, green-yellow, the rest
have dropped all their leaves, given in,
a ragged wind, frost once or twice,
the neighbours have rolled up their garden hose
and you should too, keep forgetting, sniff
what's to come in the air and yeah
here it is again

further down, the fireweed gone to seed,
walking cadavers, you think, a phrase
that caught your eye in a book
you didn't finish, their tops so ghostly grey,
highlights a pulsating redness in the undergrowth,
the osier dogwood veined, stubs

the way crows float on an upslope wind

on this side, industrial sprawl of shops, fenced yards
with barbed wire angled out, mobile homes, a motel of cabins
strung out together, abandoned burger bar, hand-drawn signs,
piles of scrap metal, idling logging trucks,
and just visible over the ridge, the wreckage
of a new subdivision, underlined by a band of birch
against the staggering conifers

STREETS ARE NOT THE MAP

this town rolled out
        a map of indecision
                edged purple with clover and vetch

we're stuck behind chip-trucks
        chemicals and fuel and civility
                the congestion in our heads

but at sunset the sky changes
        we finally learn to see
                when nobody else does

the streets are not the map
        the sky's the colour of the hillside
                and we're left looking

THIS IS IT

just what this is. the green leatherback
grasshopper clacks. a woman waters her lawn
with great globs of water from a hose.
this is the plate glass sky gone acrylic —
thick rills and runnels. just who paints
such stuff anymore? such sentiment. the workers
on what this is. the outside of a seven-storey building.
they secure what's left of the sunset. you can hear
their cordless drill from here. just what
we could take on, or, we could drive
around and around in the fine silk of it —
the clouds piling up in the distance

BLIND BIRD

the blind bird clutching one eye in its beak
flies over a long stretch of open water
black between the ice

it opened its mouth only once
when it spoke its name —
that's when its eye fell into the water

clear and aqueous, the eye slipped down
through the deep waters
until it came to rest on the bottom

a fish swam by and swallowed it

a fisherman caught the fish and gutted it
he found the eye in the entrails and held it up to the light
and was startled by what he saw

but before he could rinse it off
and pop the eye in his mouth
the blind bird swooped down and grabbed it

this is how the blind bird came to see

THIS ISN'T THE APOCALYPSE WE HOPED FOR

the trains bend and bend and follow the recursive river
and they carry everything I need

fat bees hover above satellite dishes ultraviolet in colour
while I jump in my car for more

my pockets are stuffed with receipts of corporate failure
and blister packs of synthetic gum

cloud stacked on cloud a set design
for my irresponsibility, my frustration with the weather

somewhere in the North Pacific, my plastic obsession
is being stirred into the brine by an invisible finger

PROXIMITY

my grandfather's thatch-white brow advances
from parked car to here, with a pace
just better than a plod

we build theories on the vaguest of notions:
that as a species we need to keep moving —
that this is the one condition

his determination doesn't flag
as much as the skin draped over his jaw —
slack, but not sullen

there will be one slumped in an easy-chair,
one lying in a pool of leftover violence,
and one that awakes, unaware

DECONSTRUCTING ESSO

look, he says, don't tell the guys
but that's just ballet
in the sky; I mean, Fred there
on the cherry-picker
moving slow, and the sound
you hear that? that's his air-wrench
unbolting the metal flange
that holds the letters, well
you'll see when they're gone:
one empty crossbeam holding sweet fuck all

his lit cigarette glides through the air —

and we've got to take it all in, you know
stand way back here
because of the gas fumes; can't smoke
too close

URBAN DREAMS

nothing ever happens here.

but what if one night, before dawn
you couldn't quite get back into your body?
ribcage too tight, lips pressed
and not wide open in its usual clatter,
toes — I don't know where
you normally get in
or go out — curled under
like hotel sheets tucked in at the end
                                    what then?

already the janitors have packed up their vacuums
of yesterday's lint and leftover skin,
have wiped human oil off countertops
and banisters, have Windexed kids' breath
off windowpanes

would you stay bear or crow or coyote forever?
slip out of the house before the rest awake,
make your way to the north end of town,
and gather with your cousins?

come back once in a while
to bother the garbage cans;
stare with your bright black eye
at the rest of us inside

from campfire to char pit. from the gloaming
that overcomes the forest. from receding light rays
lifting out of the canopy. from a sky that is neither
dark nor light. from streams that mumble over stones.
from the drone of mosquitoes dampened by aspen leaves

the forest empties itself.

from the faded ribbons of flagging tied to branches
of indiscriminate bush. from seismic lines cut through
trees to the right and trees to the left.
from the distant misheard plane. from the sky
that grimly glows above the trees to the north

dust hovers over the forest floor.

ahem. if you're going to go anywhere
do it by air. it'll be as if the forest
has been smoothed flat by your thumb

if you wake up in a sweat, having dreamt
wild bears or strange cries or vegetation
relax. imagine the trees pressed square and clean

into a climate-controlled mall. imagine your boss's wife
showing off their new bathroom with tiles and towels
in matching green. imagine the perfect holes

drilled into the soap dish, metallic and smooth

THIS DAY, ALL DAY, THE TREES ARE DRAPES

flowers put on lipstick for the bees, pucker

I can almost hear the p-

except the birds are hanging around, singing

when she sits down at the café, she pulls out a parachute

attends to it with needle and nylon thread

the way lips attend to the edge of a porcelain cup

dill and parsley float up out of my soup

it's a large parachute I say

you never get the same message twice she smiles

attaches triangles of rainbow to it

looks around at the sky the way birds do

GRANDSTANDING ON THE BOULEVARD

hummingbird, hover near my window

        the city was chesting out

when I went through. wore bravado
halter-topped. rail-lines and footpaths

led me to think I could leave
the industrial zones. the man at the deli

in his camouflage muscle shirt
lifted the same fork-load to his mouth

three times. he steps deliberately in pubs
when he goes to the washroom. city-wide banners

parade on lampposts. women apply a deeper shade
of blue eyeliner before dinnertime

        I need to see you
a little longer, o ruby-throat

SUNDAY MORNING DRIVE

this morning, the sky has a chance of starting something new
shaking itself loose, and why not? blows the town's debris,
the clean hills of winter, while I drive the empty streets,
slip free the last set of lights, and pull over onto crushed shale.

in the fine frieze of lichen, blotches of it on the north side
the rock big enough for two, but I'm letting it go
with a paperback, and legs dangling over, a wish
for a spaghetti-strapped summer, I see echoes everywhere —

river deltas, broccoli, a hand-drawn cross-section of a brain,
but what propels me back into the town is this:
when the chill of quartz fully enters my bones, when
an itching and aloneness envelopes me and my car and the park

HAVE A BATH

anxiety fills up the bathtub. in the water-throated gurgle,
children's voices — something's wrong for sure —
it all starts with *what if* and ends up with someone dead.
the same kind of worry
as a paring knife buried under soap suds.
we put our hand in tentatively, over and again,
this searching out of the unwanted.
what isn't a question of risk management? we send
our children off in automobiles and buses.
one minute, their smiles bobbing in the window —
but we mustn't think of it, mustn't imagine
gasoline tankers or ditches. we're not sure
how much reality we make with our minds.
turn off the water. listen carefully. see?
it's safe for now. a delicious inch of hot water on top
to stir in the suds. fingertip the black plastic handle,
draw the knife out, blade dripping. with the tip
puncture bubble after bubble. wait for the phone to ring

A NOVEL IN EXCERPTS

CHAPTER ONE

it was a pleasant fiction....................we opened....................
....................the front door....................
....
....................and the back........
..............the lilies perfuming....................
....
......followed us to the bedroom....................
....
....
....................we spoke to each other........
....
...breathing badly...with food in our mouth....through kisses....
....
....
........left pages in books...........the corners folded down........

how on a Wednesday he could wake up and spoon Cheerios
into his mouth — how cereal and cold milk could smell
just like road — how all the streets in town could unfold like a
map in his head — how going around in circles could get him
to smile in the corners — how thoughts could drop unannounced
like the police or his aunt — how decorum is the first thing to go
when a civilization implodes — how a person could grip
a steering wheel with confidence — how he could swing
into a parking spot in one fluid motion — how he could stop the car
and get out on a day like today —

gives way to breaking : gives way to absences : gives way
to whispers : gives way to the way things always are : gives way
to economy : gives way to strain : gives way to panic : gives way
to friction : gives way to glare : gives way to giving in : gives way
to slump : gives way to thinking the worst : gives way to the ends :
gives way to fingertips and tongues : gives way to the familiar :
gives way to slumber : gives way to reruns :

AFTERWORD

in the end it was all about / to a place where you could / when the
little things that / even the way you held your / a series of events
over a few / and often in the middle of / perhaps you should shut /
and what will they think / a nudge of skin on your / this
comfortable light near our / what the smallest touch can make /
here is the way / take a little bit more and / a space big enough to
hold / as familiar as your / and then we will always / here
is the way in /

NIGHT PSALM

in the dark forest of the mind
in the slime and scum of fungi
in the cool compress of slugs

grant us conks that ladder up trees

under the crush of starlight
under the prying fingers of the moon
under the phosphorescent slap of leaves

grant us refuge with the millipedes

the night rattles with ravens
the night itches with scabs
the night swallows up trains

grant us the ears of mushroom lobes

HALF-PAST CHRISTMAS

children stumble out of the Pine Centre Mall into candied
side-panels and the sliding doors of minivans
breeding wrappers and pop cans
and caked with a sullen grey

nobody pays attention to the frost
nimbly unfolding crystals on fairytale trees
now that it's half-past Christmas, and even though
under the snowbanks, it draws oxygen into the ground

the spruce with its head full of cones has dropped
seeds that have figured out the shape
of sky above — the arc of sunwarm,
punch-up gusts and winds with interlocking rain

who cares when those every year mandarin oranges
arrive in daily shipments, when rows
and rows of frozen turkeys appear
their giblets and necks neatly tucked in?

AS WE ZIGZAG THROUGH THE SCHOOLYARD GATE

the grass, bruised by the sun,
will rebound when the evening dew
is conjured out of the sky. this is a good day
to forget. we remember too much, encumbered.
we need to travel with the lightness of dogs
let off their leads, with the tilt and skew
of athletes. everything we construct
is in a tenuous balance.
there isn't a single straight tree
to measure my inclinations against.
if there wasn't so much sunshine around!
the field, clearly defined by a fence
doesn't provide any cover.
walk with me, you tug
on my free hand
our shadows suspicious
                        like clouds

AND ON EARTH ABOVE
For Phil Morrison

1.

white-headed dandelion, the wind blows

all night, into the geodesic morning —
clever wind, blows into the battens of sleep
blows into stupors
mercifully

       mostly hidden
protrusions of legs & ankles

the wind elbows resolve
peeling off love-me-love-me-not petals

shifty wind, blows underwear & swimsuits dry
blows patio umbrellas into the pool
swivels the seed points of starshine
below our line of sight

2.

across town
they have spent
the better part of the month
digging a hole

work, the measure of effort
expended
            to find a footing

concrete poured over elaborate
over geometric, over integral, over —
design & abstract & spine & skeleton

when we went there
we saw rebar, wrapped tight with wire —
could smell the faint smell of playground
in all the wet sand
& mucking about

these towers
they've built
so unevenly matched
by the sky

3.

we have rigged up
a semblance of heaven here
sat in Orkney chairs
between the good book & the bottle

waited for the city to be finished

good grass
grow in every which green

clever wind, blow cottonwood fluff
throughout the town

better to have parachutes of ideas
threaded on the wind
by spinnerets

better to have whirligigs stuck in the unmowed lawn

o backyard tree —
if we could perch so precarious
      a bird

AIN'T GONNA BE

tremblin'
tremblin'

the aspen leaves are tremblin' today
but the ghosts ain't gonna be going away

there's a man up the street with two bags
on each handle & two tied to his seat
& with two more he flies, he flies —

ain't gonna be

he's rattlin' with cans & knocking on the fence
but the gate's locked up & the dogs are a-scratchin'

ain't gonna

the cup of the holy grail is too far away
he shouts through the slats in the earth
& through the slats in the sky

gonna be going

& furthermore, & furthermore — he raises
his hand up high but the thought flies loose —
the paper leaves are rattling overhead &
blowing all around his feet

tremblin'
tremblin'

LOOKING FOR

hawkswoon
above
the stone fields

let's pull into town
leave all those places
outsourced & outskirts

—— but the moon

if we could pick
our way
between the porous

spaces that burn
with cars & grease-splatter &
half-lit diner signs

by the nightstand

would that be -
let it be -
a prayer

BLIP–BLIP

a plane bores through the long muzzle of night

is this any reason to find comfort?

somewhere before, in northern Alberta
under a sky hooded with blue
a Lubicon Cree mom points out a jet
and its perfectly white contrail
to her toddler

because   because

the story goes: tower: altitude?   pilot: classified
tower: speed?   pilot: classified   tower: heading?
pilot: classified

not a great story, I know...

blip-blip, it's off the screen

AFTERSHOCKS

I toss under the duvet
after a night of watching —
the wave comes again, a wall
I can't take my eyes off

normally I don't let myself
be affected

the voice of the newscaster punching
under belted muscle
into sciatica

the sea can mend itself
easily I think
but it doesn't relax
any part of me

I have seen this before —
pixels exploding across the screen
at the speed of disaster

the sound of the wind carries
the ancient scream of Pandora's lid
turning on its hinge

later, my eyes adjust
to the room at night —
tender photons pass
in through my window

shadows of trees swaying

ON THE PORCH

dusk and dark. the shiny beaks of the crows
are hidden in the tall trees. the magpie
has slipped into its roosting place

we could say, all is right in the universe
here and now, and not be too far off —
the moth has found the moonlight

just beyond the railing. etches small and round
in our eyes. or we could drink again
and say nothing's further from the truth

and be so close —

    if I can find you here
    then what's outside
    won't ever matter

ACKNOWLEDGEMENTS

Earlier versions of some of these poems
have appeared in the following journals
and anthologies: *The Best Canadian Poetry*
(2011), *The Enpipe Line, subTerrain, CV2,*
Event and *filling Station.* I want to thank
the editors for including my work.

Thanks to my friends, as well as the members
of my writing group in Prince George, who
have read many of these poems in their
initial drafts: Adrienne Fitzpatrick, Barb
Coupe, Beata Polanska, Crystal Smith,
Darcy Ingram, Glen Thielmann, Joanna
Smythe, Lisa Haslett, Mary MacDonald, Phil
Morrison, Rob Budde, and Vince DeCoste.

Thanks to all the wonderful people that helped
make the Sage Hill Writing Experience in 2011 a
truly great experience. Thanks to Susan Stenson
and John Lent for reading my manuscript. The
gazebo wouldn't have been the same without
you two. I would especially like to thank Al
Moritz for his generous mentorship, shaping
up the poems in this manuscript with his
precision and depth of poetic vision.

I want to thank Sharon Thesen for
taking the time to read my manuscript
and for her kind comments.

Thanks to my editor, Elizabeth Bachinsky, for her insight and creativity, who saw the book within the manuscript and helped me see it too. "Chock-A-Block" is for you, Liz.

Thanks also to my publisher, Vici Johnstone of Caitlin Press, for supporting my poetry.

More than ever before, I want to thank my wife, Linda, and my daughter, Eloise, who so generously allow me the time to write.

NOTES

On "Huntingdon Man"

In the mid 1980s, when the Sumas border
crossing near Abbotsford, BC, was undergoing
expansion, it was rumored that a surveyor
discovered a shack hidden beneath the
blackberry bushes growing in an empty lot
beside Sumas Way. Since the Canadian side of
the border is called Huntingdon, I've dubbed
the man who lived there the Huntingdon Man.

On "In Rain, In Love"

This poem began with a misheard lyric from
"Amen," a song from Jeremy Stewart's album
Plaid Clouds. The line from his song is: "the
rain pours through the roof / into the room."

On "Bring Me My Sky Canoe"

Special thanks to my friend and fellow artist,
Phil Morrison, for all the great discussions we've
had in his studio in Prince George, as well as
for our fruitful artistic collaborations. In the
fall of 2011, Phil began carving my poem "Bring
Me My Sky Canoe" into an orange Coleman
canoe. The Sky Canoe was made in memory of
Steve Switzman, who died on June 25, 2011.

For photos of the project, and to see a video-poem using the same piece, please visit my website: http://alrempel.com. Phil Morrison, owner of *Concreate Studio*, works mainly in concrete and metal, and has found different ways of incorporating text, including poetry, into his sculptures. To see more of Phil's work, please visit http://www.groopgallery.com/?page_id=634.

On "A Novel in Excerpts"

The first stanza was inspired, in part, from the line "words one spoke while breathing badly…" by Nicole Brossard, from her poem, "Soft Link 3," found in *Notebook of Roses and Civilization*, as translated by Robert Majzels and Erin Moure.

AL REMPEL

Al Rempel graduated from the University of British Columbia with a Bachelor of Science in Physics and a Bachelor of Education. In 2000, he attended the Victoria School of Writing, after which he began submitting poetry. He has since published *understories* (Caitlin Press, 2010) and *The Picket Fence Diaries* (Lipstick Press), and his writing has appeared in journals including the *Malahat Review*, *CV2*, and *Event*, as well as the anthologies *The Best Canadian Poetry 2011*, *Rocksalt*, and *4 Poets*. He has built a cabin, chopped his own firewood, and grown a garden in the bush, but now lives in Prince George with his wife and daughter.